WHY IS CHANGE SO HARD?
A Humanist Learning Systems Companion Book

By Jennifer Hancock

Published by Jennifer Hancock
Copyright 2019 by Jennifer Hancock
Published 2019

Paperback Edition
ISBN: 9781797407210
Imprint: Independently published

Title: Why is Change so Hard?
Author: Jennifer Hancock
Editor: Desiree Vogelpohl
Publisher: Humanist Learning Systems

This book is also available in as an ebook and audio
bok at most online retailers

TABLE OF CONTENTS

CHAPTER 1: INTRODUCTION 5

CHAPTER 2: THE SCIENCE OF BEHAVIORAL UNLEARNING9

CHAPTER 3: EXTINCTION BURSTS AND BLOW OUTS 13

CHAPTER 4: THE IMPORTANCE OF CONSISTENCY 17

CHAPTER 5: MANAGING CHANGE IN OURSELVES 23

CHAPTER 6: ORGANIZATIONAL CHANGE MANAGEMENT
.... 27

CHAPTER 7: THE SECRET TO ORGANIZATIONAL CHANGE
MANAGEMENT 29

CHAPTER 8: MANAGING A CULTURAL CHANGE PROCESS
.... 31

CHAPTER 9: REVIEWING THE CHANGE MANAGEMENT
PROCESS 37

CHAPTER 10: ABOUT THE AUTHOR 39

CHAPTER 1: INTRODUCTION

This is the companion book to the online course Why is Change so Hard?

What can science tell us about why people resist change? What you can do to help your staff adjust? This book discusses how to utilize behavioral psychology techniques to help overcome resistance to change in yourself and in others.

Before we can embrace change, we first have to unlearn our old ways of doing things.

Individuals and groups can benefit from this course. For more information on this course visit: https://humanistlearning.com/change1/

This book contains transcripts of the course for easy home reference.

Why Behavioral Science?

In this book we are going to discuss why we all find it so hard to change and why it's particularly difficult to create culture shifts within an organization.

To do this we are going to take an operant conditioning approach to the problem, which basically means we are going to take a behavioral psychology approach.

First, we need to learn how we as humans:

- unlearn old behaviors

- train up new behaviors

- how to use rewards and reinforcements to maximize change adoption

Specifically, we are going to learn:

- the most effective unlearning techniques

- what the process of change is really like and what to expect

- how to train yourself and others to embrace change over time

When you understand this, it becomes easier to not get frustrated with the pace of change. Always remember, your staff, as well meaning as they are, have to extinguish the old ways of doing things in order to adopt the new ways of doing things. Which means, they are going to go through an extinction burst or blow out, which I will describe later.

Failure to manage the extinction burst process is why most attempts to change the culture fail. Leaders don't recognize that staff resistance is really just a manifestation of an extinction burst and so tend to give up too soon instead of seeing the collective staff blow out through to completion.

This knowledge is useful in a variety of situations. It's the same process I teach in the anti-bullying programs I offer. It also helps you to understand and manage most of your interpersonal relationships.

~~~~~

CHAPTER 2: THE SCIENCE OF BEHAVIORAL UNLEARNING

The key to understanding why it is so hard to get people to embrace change is to understand how we unlearn behaviors. It turns out we as humans unlearn the same way all animals unlearn things. To do this intentionally, there is really only one protocol that seems to work. It's called "Extinguishing a Behavior."

You eliminate the reward. This causes a behavioral escalation as the animal tries to get their reward back. If the reward continues to be denied, eventually the animal will escalate to the point the behavior becomes almost constant. This is known as an extinction burst or blow out. If the reward continues to be denied despite desperate attempts by the animal to get their reward back - they will eventually give up.

There are more than 7 decades of research into this topic and there have been no counter examples found. This is considered established science by behavioral psychologists. All behavioral unlearning follows this pattern. The only thing that varies is how bad the escalation, extinction burst or blow out is.

Because this is considered established science I will not be citing specific studies. Instead, I will be describing how to use this knowledge to help you improve outcomes. If you are curious about the research, here are some links to scholarly articles for you to review on the subject.

- Behavioral extinction
  (https://scholar.google.com/scholar?hl=en&as_sdt=0%2C10&q=behavioral+extinction&btnG=&oq=behavio)

- Operant conditioning
  (https://scholar.google.com/scholar?hl=en&as_sdt=0%2C10&q=operant+conditioning+&btnG=)

The Extinguishing a Behavior Protocol:

In order to unlearn a habitualized rewarded behavior, you have to do several things. These steps are what are known as extinguishing a behavior and are a standard operant conditioning technique.

- Stop rewarding the unwanted behavior

- Increase the cost associated with performing the unwanted behavior

- Ride out the blow by being 100% consistent in not providing a reward despite repeatedly more aggressive attempts to get a reward

- Reward the behavior you do want (provide an alternative way to get a reward)

- Nip in the bud any future attempts to re-establish the unwanted behavior

When you try to get yourself or a group of people to stop doing one thing and start doing something new, you have to first extinguish the old behavior so that you CAN train up the new behavior. Failure to do this will cause you to fail.

~~~~~

CHAPTER 3: EXTINCTION BURSTS AND BLOW OUTS

The reason it is so hard to get unwanted behaviors to stop is because people resist change. Instinctually. Even if they want to change, they will resist. In order to give yourself the best chance of success, it is important to understand exactly what the extinction process is like, what an extinction burst is and how they manifest.

Anyone who has been addicted to something like cigarettes, alcohol, or drugs will tell you that it's not easy to quit. Habits are really hard to break.

For example, I drive the same way to my son's school and the same way back. I have been doing this for a couple of years. If I drop my son off at school and decide to go to the market before returning home - I have to exert quite a bit of mental energy to ensure I turn left instead of my normal right. If I don't pay attention, I will drive myself home, as is my habit, instead of driving to the market. I can get myself to the market, but I have to make a conscious effort to overcome my habitual driving patterns to do so. Anything you do on autopilot - including driving a car - is a learned behavior. You can unlearn it, but it takes effort.

When it comes to unlearning a routine or workplace process, we are dealing with the same thing. These are habits. We do them because "they've always worked." It's not that we don't understand that this other way might be better, it's more that it's so HARD to break old habits. It's easier to keep doing what you are doing than unlearn an old way of doing it.

This is why some of us keep using old computers at home way past the time we should. It's easier than dealing with learning something new. In order for us to give up the old way – it pretty much has to stop working entirely! Which in our operant conditioning terms means that we stopped receiving the reward, which is step one of the protocol.

But there is another reason why it's so hard to give up our old ways. And that is the behavioral response known as "the extinction burst." An extinction burst is what happens when you eliminate "the reward." Everyone does it and all animals do it. It's kind of an instinctual thing.

An Example of an Extinction Burst or Blow Out

Let's say that every day at 3 pm you walk to the vending machine in your office, put money into it, press some buttons and get a candy bar. And let's say this is your regular afternoon routine and you've been doing it for over 2 years. What happens if one day you go to the vending machine, as is your habit, put in your money, press the buttons and … nothing happens? What do you do?

Most people - push more buttons. They may shake the machine. They will escalate their behavior to try and get their candy bar. Almost no one, when confronted with a broken vending machine, will accept that the machine is broken and just walk away. Almost everyone will escalate their behavior for a while before we give up. This is exactly what we expect to see happen based on a behavioral extinction model. The escalation is expected. Everyone, even the little old nice lady who has nothing bad to say about anyone - will "fight" with a broken vending machine.

The only question is how bad will people resist the reality of the broken vending machine before giving up. Some people give up quickly, others will get more aggressive. But everyone will escalate their behavior before they give up.

Everyone does this. The reward is denied or removed, we escalate the behavior. If the reward continues to be denied, we will eventually give up. This is how all habits are broken. It doesn't matter what the behavior is. This is what the process of unlearning is like. Properly understanding this process directly impacts your ability to get yourself and your organization to adapt to change.

~~~~~

CHAPTER 4: THE IMPORTANCE OF CONSISTENCY

Because consistency is so important to the whole "why people resist change" phenomenon, we are going to discuss it in more detail.

When we break a habit, we all go through an extinction burst. The escalation of behavior that is the extinction burst or blow out follows a very predictable pattern. Once we understand what is happening, it becomes much easier to control it.

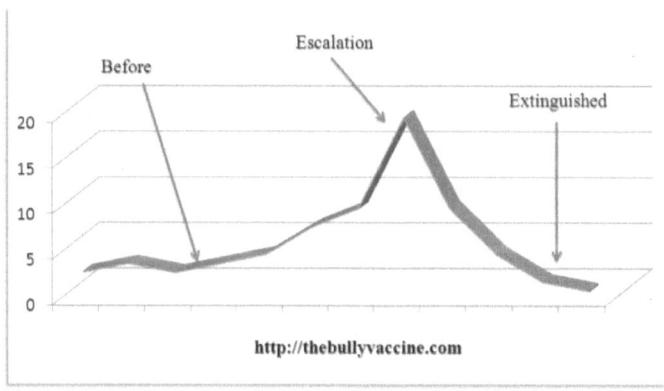

The above graph shows the typical behavioral escalation pattern of a blow out or extinction burst. We have some level of behavior happening. When the reward is removed, the behavior escalates. If the reward continues to be denied, the behavior escalates more and more. If the reward continues to be denied, eventually, the animal will give up and stop. Kind of.

FOR EXAMPLE:

Let's imagine that there is a rat in a cage. And every time it presses a lever - it gets a treat. There is some level of behavior that is happened. An average number of lever presses per hour. If the lever stops giving the rat a treat, the rat will press the lever more and more. Until it's pressing the lever almost constantly. This is the blow out phase or extinction burst. If the lever continues to not give a reward, the rat will eventually give up and stop pressing the lever. This is what we call behavioral extinction. The problem is that as long as the lever is there, the rat will occasionally press it. Just at a lower rate than it was previously. Just in case the lever starts working again.

What I want you to understand is that every behavior being extinguished in every animal ever studied, including humans, follows this pattern. There is some level of behavior, the reward is removed, the behavior escalates until, eventually, the behavior extinguishes - kind of.

How bad the behavior gets depends on how long the behavior has been established and how naturally aggressive the individual is. If it is a new behavior, we give it up quickly. If it is established, we don't. If we are naturally aggressive, we will probably fight more to get our reward back than people who are more mild mannered. But all of us will escalate before stopping.

What happens if we don't complete the extinction process?

Behavioral extinction requires consistent removal of reward. It is only if the reward is well and truly gone, that we get behavioral extinction. If the reward returns, the behavior returns. And it doesn't just return - it returns in a worse form.

What is happening during an extinction process is that the individual is escalating their behavior in an attempt to get their reward back. If they get their reward back, what they have learned is - in order to get their reward, they just have to be more aggressive. If you give in and start rewarding the behavior again, instead of the original status quo level of behavior, we get a new more aggressive level of behavior. Because we will have essentially taught our subject that if they want their reward, they need to be more aggressive.

In most cases and most situations, this is the exact opposite of what we want people to learn. We want people to learn that it doesn't matter how aggressive they get, they aren't getting their reward back. To teach this we need to be consistent.

USING BULLYING AS AN EXAMPLE:
We see this escalating dynamic play out most clearly in bullying situations. We have some level of bullying behavior. The target stops responding, the bullies escalate, and the target starts responding again. This is what we call - variable reinforcement - meaning sometimes the individual gets their reward and

sometimes they don't. This is a natural pattern we fall into when we are dealing with aggressive individuals.

The dynamic that plays out is that every time we stop responding the way a bully likes, they get more aggressive trying to get us to respond to them again. We think, what we were just doing didn't work, it made it worse and it did. So we start responding again. What the bully has just learned is - I just need to be more obnoxious to get my reward. What we see with bullying is a series of failed extinction attempts.

The way to get out of that cycle is to be consistent. It doesn't matter how obnoxious or aggressive the bully gets, they must not be rewarded ever. Only with consistent removal of reward do we get to extinction. If we variably reinforce, meaning sometimes we respond and sometimes we don't we are inadvertently teaching the subject that getting more obnoxious works.

Applying this to change management

When we apply this known dynamic to the problem of change management, we can see that we have some level of previous behavior going on. In order to get people to give up their old behavior, we have to stop allowing the old ways to work. Otherwise they will continue to do the old way.

When we stop allowing the old way to work, people get upset. They are in "denial" and they get more aggressive to try and get things to go back to the way they were before. How aggressive they get depends on their basic personality. Eventually, if things really have changed, they will give up and adopt or quit.

What I want you to understand is that this dynamic is the main reason why it is so hard for people to embrace change. What is critical to understand is that in order to get the unlearning to occur so that staff can embrace what is new, you have to complete the extinction process.

If you give in before the old behavior is extinguished and you allow people to go back to the old ways of doing things, then you have not only failed to create the change you wanted, you have also pretty much ensured that the next attempt to create change will be met with even more resistance because – hey, our protestations worked last time!

~~~~~

CHAPTER 5: MANAGING CHANGE IN OURSELVES

Before we get into discussing what it will take to manage change within an organization or a group, let's talk about what it takes to create change within ourselves.

Change is hard. It's hard because most of our behavior is unconscious and habitual or instinctual.

The Social Psychologist Jon Haidt in his book *The Happiness Hypothesis* – talks about the divided self. The metaphor he uses is that you imagine yourself riding an elephant. You are the thinking, rational, choosing aspect of the behavior. You are the rider. Your unconscious brain is the elephant. You are telling the elephant where to go, kind of. But the elephant has his own ideas on where to go and what to do.

If your brain is made up of a rider and an elephant – the rider is only about 1% of the brain. The rest of the brain is the elephant running on instinct. You have some ability to tell your instinctual elephant where to go through conscious choice, but if you really want to ensure your inner elephant behaves in certain ways, it's actually better if you can make those behaviors instinctual.

When we return to what this means in terms of how we embrace change, or don't, we see that it isn't enough to want to change. We have to actually train our inner elephant to behave the way we want. And training an elephant isn't easy. It can be done, but it takes time. So give yourself that time.

Practice the New Behavior

What do you do with that time? You practice the new behaviors you want your elephant to learn! And in some cases, that means helping them unlearn old behaviors first. The key is to practice. Remove the rewards for the old behaviors and reward the new ones. Repeatedly and consistently.

The good news, according to research by Australian researchers Megan Oaten and Ken Chang (http://blog.bufferapp.com/what-the-research-on-habit-formation-reveals-about-willpower-and-overall-well-being) is that the more you practice at something, the more willpower you have, the easier it becomes. Practicing good habits is a lot like working out a muscle. The more you do it, the stronger it gets. So give it time and keep practicing.

Be Compassionate with Yourself

The next thing is to be compassionate with yourself. Understanding that your instincts are to not only resist but to actively work to go back to your old ways of doing things actually makes it easier to stick with the new ways. Whenever you get the old instinctual urges, you can accept them but not act upon them.

And if you do act upon them, you don't have to beat yourself up for lacking willpower because your failure wasn't about willpower. It was about habit.

You just have to keep at it and keep trying and keep practicing and strengthen both the new behavior and your willpower at the same time. Eventually, if you give yourself the time, dedicate yourself to practicing the new behavior, remove the temptation and the rewards for the old behavior, then you will create change.

Dieting as an Example

I lost about 20 lbs. It took me about 1 ½ years to do that.

What I can tell you is that giving myself that amount of time and not trying to change my eating habits overnight by fad dieting allowed me the time I needed to practice new eating habits so that they became new habits. Taking a slower approach is what helped me to succeed. And most studies on dieting backs that up.

Sure, you can lose weight on a fad diet, but you are more likely to gain that weight back and then some if you do it quickly compared to if you approach weight loss as a matter of habit formation. Your urges to go back to your old eating habits are normal and do not need to be acted upon.

When you approach change as a matter of habit formation, you are aware that unlearning a habit takes time and replacing it with a new habit also takes time. So you are more likely to put the time in the habit formation process and thus be more likely to succeed at not reverting to your old habits once you complete your change process. And the reason for this is because by taking the time to address habit formation, you will have completed the extinction process as part of this approach, and because your new habits will be actual habits!

The more you succeed at changing your behavior, the more your resistance to change lessens, because you are also learning that resistance is futile. Every time you successfully complete a behavioral extinction, you are learning and strengthening what we normally call willpower, as your brain learns that it doesn't matter how much it resists change, it's not getting it's reward back.

This is why the advice is often to start with something small. Give yourself a win and then chose something else to change. Every time you succeed, even with a small change, you make the next change process easier.

~~~~~

CHAPTER 6: ORGANIZATIONAL CHANGE MANAGEMENT

Now let's transfer this knowledge to organizational change management. The fact that your staff is going through an extinction burst whenever an attempt is made to change the culture explains a lot.

Leaders rarely recognize that staff resistance is really just a manifestation of an extinction burst and so they tend to misinterpret what is actually happening. We wish people would be like robots that we can reprogram, but they aren't. They are humans. It's not unusual for leaders to get cranky and self-righteous when their staff do not embrace the changes requested.

This manifests as an attitude problem on behalf of the leaders seeking change. And yes, it does make things worse and makes change less likely. Mostly because this – everyone else is too stupid to understand how brilliant these changes are going to be - attitude is very condescending. It's also not a compassionate approach to your employees who have to unlearn the old ways of doing things before they can embrace the new.

No wonder they resist. Focus on helping them unlearn their old habits and you will be much more successful.

Don't Give Up Too Soon

The other problem this cultural extinction process causes is that it frustrates leaders so much, they end up giving up too soon instead of seeing the collective staff blow out through to completion.

In other words – not knowing that whenever you try to change something you are going to trigger an escalation of resistance that leads to an extinction burst causes leaders to a) not deal effectively with the reality of what it takes to create change, and b) give up on the change process way too soon.

Now that you know to expect an extinction burst, let's talk about how this is going to impact how we approach change management.

First, extinguishing a behavior is a process that takes time. You can't just dictate a change and have it implemented. You have to plan for the time it will take for your staff to adjust to and embrace the changes. This is the sort of thing that can take months. So give it the time it requires.

Second, don't require everyone to change all at the same time. Identify those who are least likely to resist change and train them first. Let them prove the concept of how it works and how much better it is than the old way.

This allows you to eliminate the possibility of an organizational pushback against your proposed changes by not starting with the very people most likely to rebel.

~~~~~

CHAPTER 7: THE SECRET TO ORGANIZATIONAL CHANGE MANAGEMENT

Here is the secret to the entire thing.

If you are going to create true change within your organization, you can't just train people on the new processes. There has to be an ongoing effort over time.

The first problem change agents encounter is that they think they need to get everyone to agree to the change in order to create the change. This is what I call the buy-in fallacy.

You Don't Need Everyone

The reality is that you don't need everyone.

You only need a couple of people in each department to get started. These early adopters, if nurtured properly, will help create the conditions necessary for the second wave of adopters to join in.

We humans are tribal animals. We have a strong instinctual desire to adhere to the cultural norms of our tribe. This means that changing those cultural norms is very hard.

But this "herd" mentality is a double-edged sword. It's annoying when it causes us to not do the right thing but can also be harnessed to encourage people to do the right thing. All that is really needed is someone willing to set a new example or a new cultural expectation.

When you want to create cultural change in an organization or within a group of people, you need to find some early adopters who are willing to step outside the "keep your head" down culture that tends to dominate and actively and visibly step forward to adopt the new way of doing things. This is why it is so essential to get your response to these "early adopters" right!

~~~~~

CHAPTER 8: MANAGING A CULTURAL CHANGE PROCESS

Let's imagine that you just trained your staff up on new processes to eliminate bullying and harassment in the workplace.

All organizations suffer from this to one extent or another and it's incredibly hard to fix. Why? Because the norms, acculturated from the time we are children, discourage the active reporting required to get bullying and harassment behaviors to actually stop.

Most organizations have some form of anti-harassment training. And it's great, but it almost always has almost no discernible impact on employee behaviors. Actually, this is true of almost all ethical training programs.

If you actually want to create change and have your training stick, you have to understand what that change process is and especially why your early adopters will make or break your change process.

Early Adopters

Once you complete your new training, expect only a handful of people to actually take to the training and do what you encourage them to do. Most won't and that's ok.

Your job in this stage is to nurture and support your early adopters so they don't give up. This is especially true when you are trying to extinguish something like harassment and a culture that inadvertently enables bullying.

The early adopters are putting their necks out for you and that means that they will likely experience a backlash from their fellow employees. You need to help them through this and see the extinction process they trigger for what it is, normal resistance to change, and encourage them to continue what they are doing until the resistance to change is extinguished. If you fail to do this at this stage, you will not be able to move on to the next stage of cultural transformation. Because if you fail to adequately support the early adopters, they will give up and no one else will even attempt it and the resistors will have learned that resistance works.

At each level you need people willing to work on this together and see it through. You also need to make it clear that they have a point person to go to IF/WHEN they encounter problems implementing the changes you have requested.

This is important because it's often the managers who lead the resistance to change and you need your early adopters to be supported, even if their direct managers don't support them in this. It's actually a good idea to have people in support roles identified, trained, and in place before you even begin to ask staff to adopt something new.

The 2nd Wave of Change

Assuming you are able to encourage early adopters to embrace the change and assuming that they are successful with the changes, it should trigger the second wave of cultural transformation. This is when most everyone else will jump on board.

When people see that not only does this new way of doing things work, but that it is supported and more importantly, that people who have taken on these new changes are actively and openly rewarded for doing so, this will create a shift in attitudes for the majority of your staff.

At this stage you will have people asking you to participate in the change process you are implementing. They will be encouraging one another to adopt the changes and together will create a new cultural norm.

It is important at this stage to help support each individual as they go through their individual extinction process so that they can adapt the new change. As eager as people are to embrace change, they will revert back to the old ways of doing things if given an opportunity because the old way was a habit. And it's hard to break a habit.

It's fairly easy to support just the few early adopters through this process, but scaling up to support for the second wave is a bit harder. This is why it is essential to have good processes in place and to make sure you continue to support management as they adjust to this new way of doing things and the new expectations staff have of their managers.

As a change manager, I like to take this one department at a time. That way I am not overwhelmed and I can support each unit of the organization as they adjust and become independently able to sustain the cultural change. Once that team has successfully made the transition I start focusing on other departments that are asking me to assist them to create a similar change with their team.

For me, the best way to manage the second wave is to stagger them and keep building upon each success. Don't try to do this all at once. You will end up being spread too thin and won't be able to provide the necessary support required to create lasting change.

What to do with Those who Lag Behind

Finally, you will need to decide what you want to do about those who lag behind. How much time are you going to give them to adapt to the new cultural norms of the group? Different people react to change in different ways.

When you stagger your transformation process, you provide space and time for most people to adapt to that change, giving them the time they need to "blow out" and give up and adapt.

The problem is, even with all the evidence that the change has been beneficial, you will still have some people who will insist that this newfangled way of behaving just won't work. This isn't too much of a problem when the lagger is a staff member. At some point the transition is complete and they either get with the program or get fired. It's not pleasant, but that's what happens.

The situation is much harder when the lagger is a manager. You need to be prepared for what you plan to do if a manager refuses to change.

Without the full support of upper management for whatever cultural shift you are envisioning, you won't be able to tackle the problem of lagging managers, and their continued presence will create ongoing problems and prevent full implementation of the cultural shift you are trying to create.

Don't let this get you down. The fact you are now at this point is a good sign. If you keep at the other elements of change, eventually it will become evident to everyone that the lagging person is a problem and peer pressure will either be enough to get them to change or it will make it clear they need to leave. Remind yourself this is another manifestation of an extinction burst. If it was easy, it wouldn't ever be a problem.

Regardless, you will find that you rarely have to confront these individuals directly if you keep pushing and making progress with other individuals. Eventually the pressure on those lagging will become so great that change will be demanded and will occur.

Or, the lagging manager will start behaving so badly as part of their extinction burst that they get themselves fired. I've seen both happen.

Change managers need to be prepared for either eventuality and a decision should be made by upper management on what to do about lagging managers as they have the power to subvert the entire process and they may need to actively be asked to leave if they continue to resist.

~~~~~

CHAPTER 9: REVIEWING THE CHANGE MANAGEMENT PROCESS

In order to create change, you first have to plan for and manage the extinction process for the old behavior. To do that you have to be consistent over time. If you vary in your commitment and consistency, you will make change less likely to occur.

We should respond to the resistance to change with compassionate non-compliance. Meaning – when someone resists change, we don't get upset or take it personally. We understand that this resistance is natural and while a bit annoying, just part of the process. Getting mad or angry with a person who resists change makes things worse and makes the person resisting change dig into their position more.

We can encourage the extinction process to play out over time by not allowing the old ways to work anymore. The main goal is to maintain this course of action through the extinction burst until the behavior we don't want is extinguished.

Unlearning Old Behaviors Requires Consistency

To unlearn old behaviors we need to be consistent and compassionate with ourselves and others as we first resist change and then unlearn our old habits to learn new habits. Habits take a while to form and they take a while to unlearn. If you don't give yourself the time for this to happen, it won't happen.

You need to allocate the appropriate amount of time to practice the new behavior so you can replace the old one. And this time needs to include the time it takes to unlearn the old behavior.

Mostly, you are going to need to have a strategy or plan on how to roll out your proposed changes over time so that you have the best chance of having them not only adopted, but sticking.

Change as Habit Formation

Change is hard. If you think about change as a matter of habit formation, you will be more successful precisely because it's a more realistic approach than assuming you can just reprogram a human.

The key is to have compassion for yourself and for others and to always consider yourself a work in progress. Always look for ways to improve what you do. It isn't easy to change, but the more you practice, the easier it gets.

~~~~~

CHAPTER 10: ABOUT THE AUTHOR

Jennifer Hancock is a mom, author of several books, and founder of Humanist Learning Systems. Jennifer is unique in that she was raised as a freethinker and is considered one of the top speakers and writers in the world of Humanism today. Her professional background is varied including stints in both the for profit and non-profit sectors. She has served as Director of Volunteer Services for the Los Angeles SPCA, sold international franchise licenses for a biotech firm, was the Manager of Acquisition Group Information for a ½ billion-dollar company and served as the executive director for the Humanists of Florida. When she became a mother, she decided to stay at home, but that didn't last long. Shortly after her son was born, she published her first book, The Humanist Approach to Happiness: Practical Wisdom. Her speaking and teaching business coalesced into the founding of Humanist Learning Systems which provides online personal and professional development training in humanistic business management and science-based harassment training that actually works.

More Learning from Jennifer Hancock

OTHER BOOKS BY JENNIFER HANCOCK

- The Humanist Approach to Happiness

- Jen Hancock's Handy Humanism Handbook

- The Bully Vaccine

- The Humanist Approach to Grief and Grieving

- How to Win Arguments Without Arguing

- Ending Harassment & Retaliation in the Workplace

- Why Bullies Bully & How to Stop Them Using Science

- Reality Based Decision Making for Effective Strategy Development

- Planning for Personal Success

- Why Conflict Management Doesn't Work When the Problem is Bullying

- Why Bullies Bully and How to Stop Them Using Science

- How to Handle Cranky Customer Problems Using Behavioral Science

- How to De-escalate Conflicts Using Behavioral Science

- Bridging the Generation Divide: Millennials vs. Boomers

- How to Talk to Your Child's School About Bullying

Courses taught by Jennifer Hancock

- Workplace Bullying for HR professionals

- Living Made Simpler

- An Introduction to Humanism

- Socratic Jujitsu: How to Win Arguments Without Arguing

- Why Conflict Resolution Doesn't Work When the Problem is Bullying

- Bridging the Generational Divide: Millennials vs. Boomers

- Ending Harassment and Retaliation in the Workplace

- Reality Based Decision Making for Effective Strategy Development

- How to De-escalate Conflicts Using Behavioral Science

- Why is Change so Hard?

- Principles of Humanistic Management

- 7 Sins of Staff Management

- How to Handle Cranky Customer Problems

- New Manager Orientation

- Humanist Group Leadership Lessons

- Sexual harassment training that works – general

- Sexual harassment training that works – AB 1825

- Stop Bullying in our Workplace – Staff Training

- Sexual Harassment Compliance Training

- No Fear Act Training

- Planning for Personal Success!

- Talking to your child about death

- The Bully Vaccine Toolkit

- How to talk to your child's school about bullying

- Why Bullies Bully & How to Stop Them

- How to Prevent Passive Aggressive People from Wreaking Havoc in the Workplace

Connect with Me Online:

· Twitter: http://twitter.com/#!/JentheHumanist

· Facebook: http://www.facebook.com/JentheHumanist

· Or sign up for my mailing list: http://eepurl.com/c3LuI